GINN HISTORY PATCH SERIES: THE ROMANS

AQUAE SULIS

BY BARRY CUNLIFFE

Illustrations by Martin Simmons

GINN AND COMPANY LTD
18 BEDFORD ROW LONDON WC1R 4EJ

AQUAE SULIS

The Roman name of Bath, Aquae Sulis, suggests two things: that the settlement was notable for its springs and that a deity known as Sulis featured prominently in the religious life of the community. Both of these facts have been dramatically proved by archaeological discoveries made during the last three hundred years. But although it is true to say that we know a great deal of the principal monumental buildings of the town, the nature of the rest of the settlement is difficult to establish. One reason is that since Bath is a town of considerable architectural merit its eighteenth century buildings are vigorously protected and very little redevelopment of the ancient centre takes place. Archaeologists must, therefore, be content with limited excavation, often carried out under difficult conditions, in the cellars beneath standing buildings.

The origins of the town

The Roman settlement lies on a sloping spur of land bordered on the east and south by the river Avon. At this point the Fosse Way, the Roman road leading from the vicinity of Isca (Exeter) to Lindum (Lincoln) crosses the river. Other roads also converge here: from Calleva (Silchester) and Londinium (London), from Poole Harbour and to the port on the mouth of the river Avon at Abouae (Sea Mills). The Fosse Way began as a military frontier road constructed within a few years of the invasion of AD 43 to provide easy communications between permanently based garrisons. It may well be that a military base was established at or near Aquae Sulis. A number of early military tombstones have been found, such as that erected for the cavalryman Lucius Vitellius Tancinus.

Whatever its Roman origins, there can be no doubt that it was the great mineral water springs that

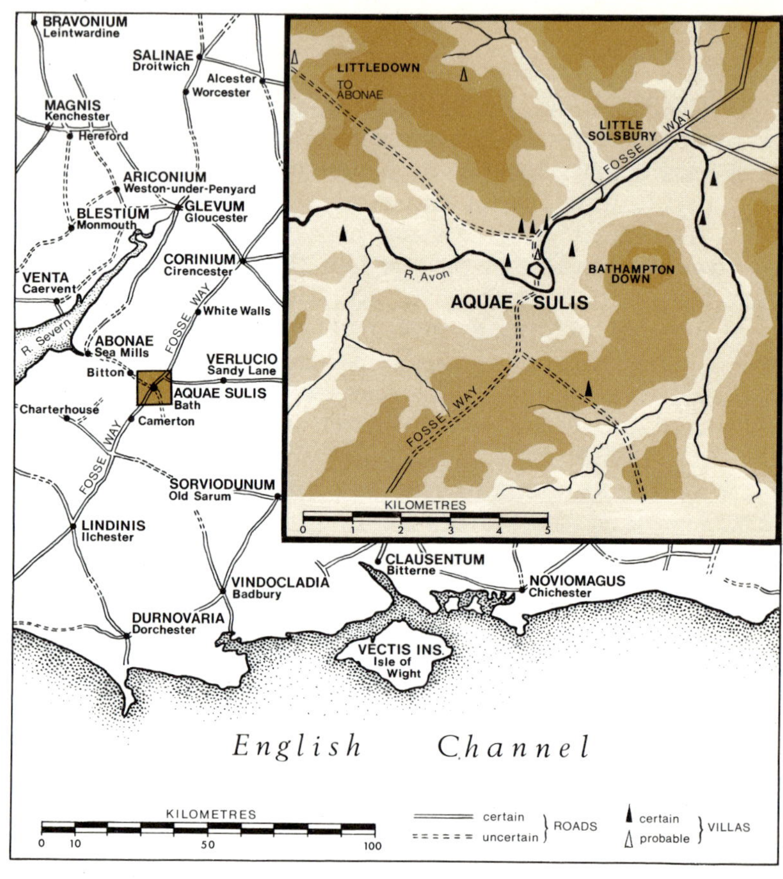

Map showing Aquae Sulis in relation to south-western Britain

attracted Roman developers, for in what is now the centre of the town nearly two and a quarter million litres of mineral water, at a temperature of about 50°C, gush out of the ground daily. Such a dramatic natural phenomenon cannot have passed unrevered in the pre-Roman period, nor were the Romans slow to develop it. The spring was exploited in two ways: it featured as a focal point in a great temple complex erected to serve its presiding deity, and the waters were led into a huge bathing establishment used partly for pleasure and partly to provide a cure for illnesses.

The temple to Sulis Minerva

The temple building now lies beneath the main road called Stall Street, just north-east of the Pump Room, some four metres below the present street level. From the many inscriptions found in the town from time to time it is clear that the goddess worshipped here was Sulis Minerva, a combination of the old Celtic deity's name of Sulis with the Roman name Minerva, goddess of, among other things, healing. Her temple was built on a high concrete podium or platform measuring 10 metres by 20 metres, reached by a flight of steps leading up to the short east side. From the fragments of the superstructure recovered from excavations over the last two hundred and fifty years we know that the temple front consisted of four large fluted Corinthian columns supporting a decorated triangular pediment, see page 6. The columns fronted a porch area, behind which was the cella, or principal chamber, of the temple. Columns like those of the front were continued along the sides and back of the cella, against

Gilded bronze head of the goddess Minerva from a cult statue found in Bath in 1727, see colour slide (1)

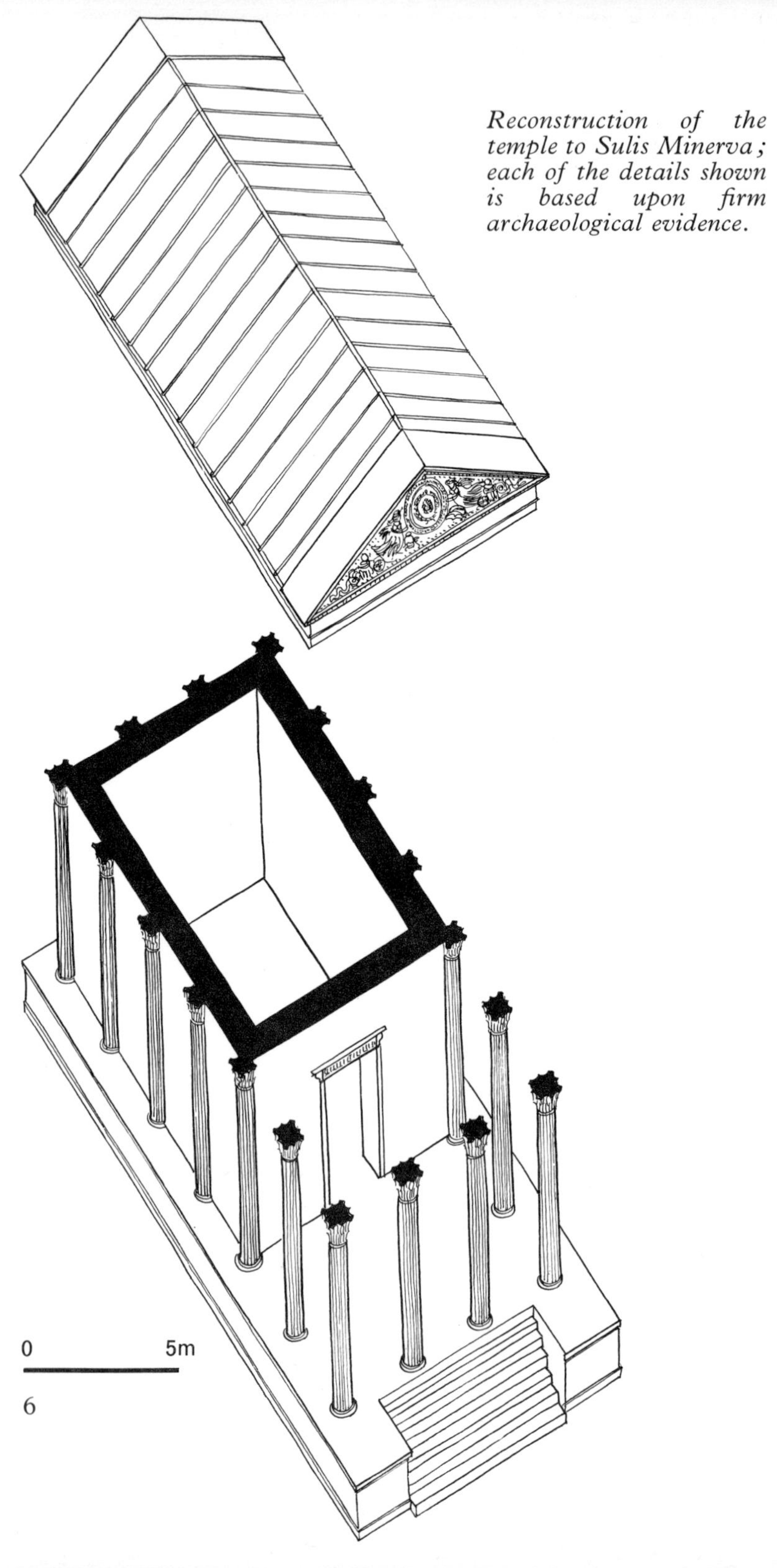

Reconstruction of the temple to Sulis Minerva; each of the details shown is based upon firm archaeological evidence.

the wall to which they were attached. Between the columns flanking the porch was a stone balustrade. Part of one of the columns, now on show in the museum at Bath, still bears the slot cut into its base mouldings so that the low balustrade could neatly abut to it.

The most dramatic feature of the temple then, as now, was its elaborately carved limestone pediment, of which about a half has survived. In the centre is a shield wreathed with oak leaves and held aloft by two winged Victories in true Roman manner. On the shield is carved a glowering gorgon's head with snakes in the hair, but instead of being female, as the gorgon is in classical mythology, it is shown as a male with billowing moustaches. These and his lentoid (lens-shaped) eyes, frowning brow and wedge-shaped nose are all features common in pre-Roman Celtic art. At Aquae Sulis, then, the classical idea of the gorgon has been transformed by the strong local artistic spirit into an interpretation of a Celtic male. Such a combination of Celtic and Roman tradition is a fitting centre-piece for a temple dedicated to Sulis Minerva. The remainder of the pediment is equally finely carved with fabulous sea creatures, called

7

Tritons in the lower corners, and beneath the shield an owl and a helmet—symbols usually associated with the goddess Minerva.

The temple itself formed a focal point of the religious plan. It lay in the centre of a substantial precinct measuring 78 metres by 52 metres, surrounded by a colonnaded walk. A visitor to the temple would have entered the precinct through a monumental double-arched gate in the centre of the east wall and would immediately have been faced with the main front of the temple, but between him and the temple lay the great sacrificial altar where the public rites of the temple would have been performed. The altar would originally have consisted of a solid mass of masonry about 1·3 metres high and probably about 3 metres square. Its corners were elaborately carved with a deity on each face. One of the corners, found in 1790, shows Hercules Bibax, the drinking Hercules, on one side with Jupiter on the adjacent face. Another corner, much better preserved, was found in the recent excavation in 1965 beneath the cellar floor of the Pump Room. One side shows a naked Bacchus holding a staff in one hand and pouring a libation to a panther squatting at his feet. His partner on the other side of the block is a heavily draped female deity who is shown holding a cornucopia and pouring a libation from an upturned vase. A third corner is known, built into the buttress of a church at Compton Dando, 11 kilometres from Bath. Though very weathered, it is still possible to recognize the carvings of two gods, one of whom is Apollo playing a lyre.

The altar then was a dramatic centre-piece in the temple layout. It would have been made even more impressive by the two statues which, it is believed, stood in front of it. The base for one of these was found in the excavation of 1965, still standing in its original position on the sandstone slabs paving the precinct. It was inscribed with the words DEAE SULI, LUCIUS MARCIUS MEMOR, HARUSP, D.D. meaning 'To the Goddess Sulis, Lucius Marcius Memor, Augurer, gave this gift.' Memor's profession, that of a high-

*Corner block of the altar
depicting the god Bacchus*

*Corner block of the altar
carved with a female deity*

*A statue base found in
front of the altar put up
by Lucius Marcius Memor*

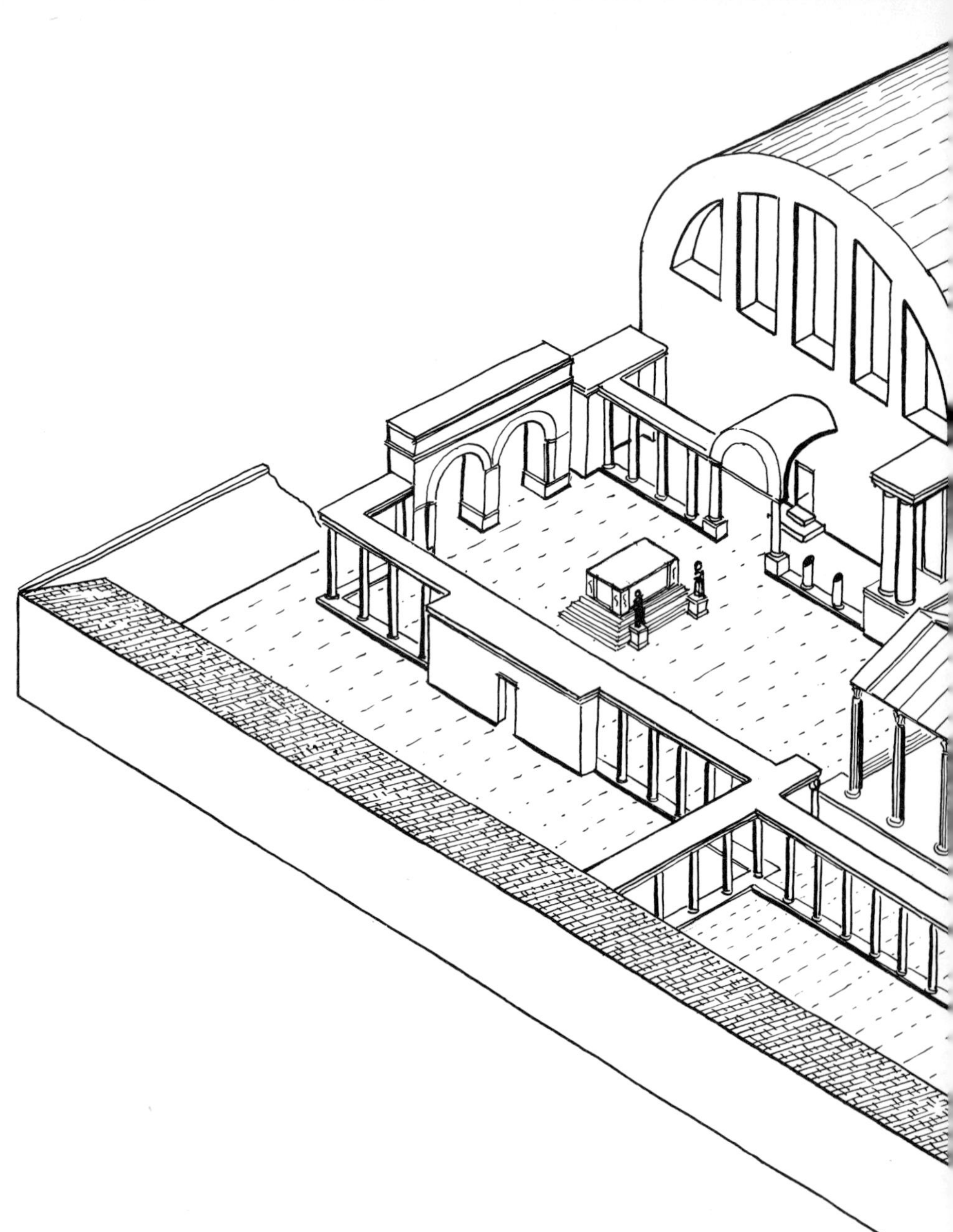

The general arrangement of the temple precinct can be largely reconstructed from the archaeological evidence. It is shown here in the latest stage of its development, after the original layout had received many alterations.

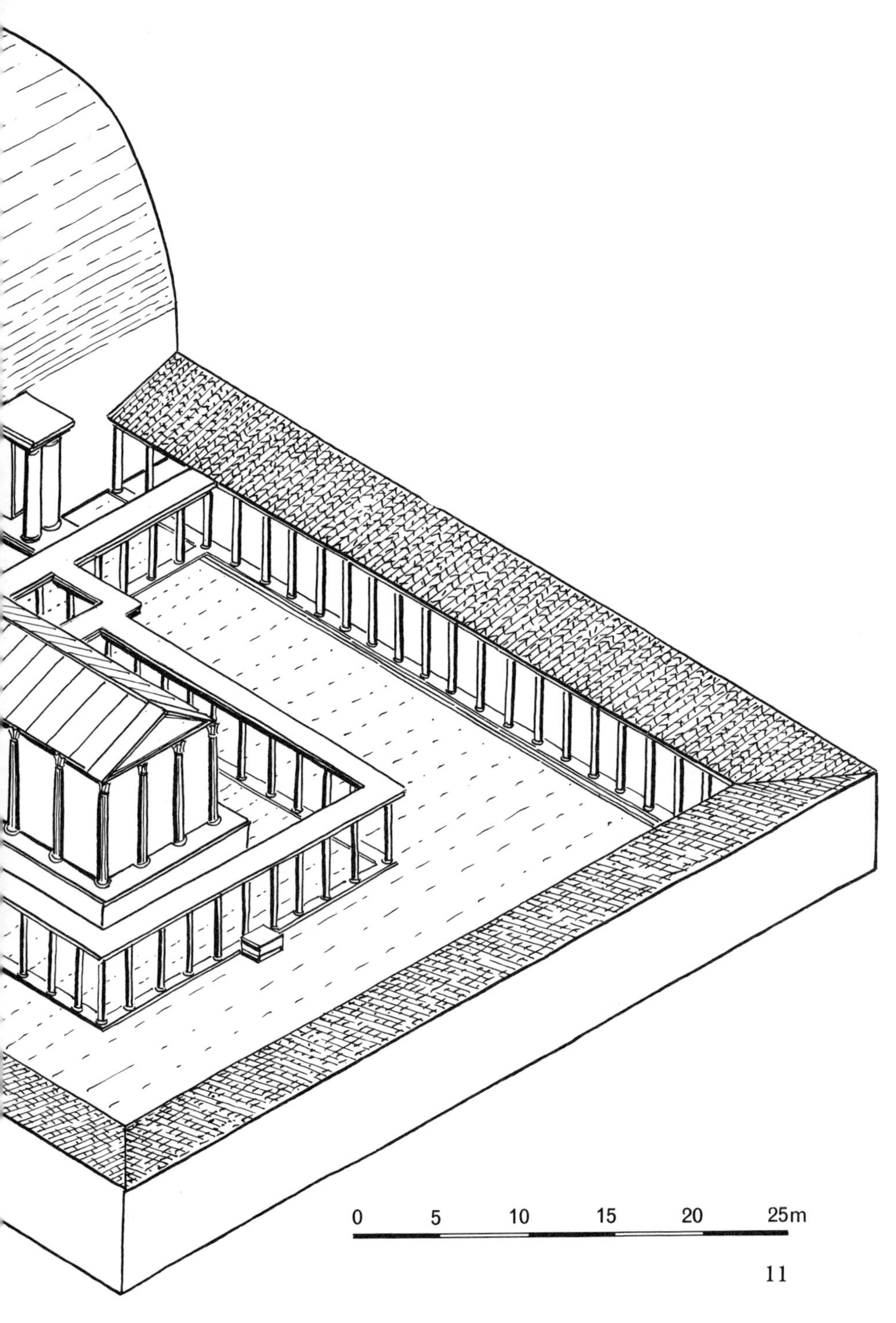

0
5
10
15
20
25m

ranking augurer or soothsayer, is particularly interesting. He would have been responsible for officiating in the temple rituals, possibly on this very altar, by cutting open the animals offered as sacrifices and examining their entrails for omens by which he could foretell the future. He would also have based his prophecies on the way in which birds flew across the sky. For a man of such skill to be present in Aquae Sulis is an indication of the high regard in which the temple was held.

The features so far described are rare in Britain but can be found among many of the temples in Gaul, Spain and Italy. Where the temple at Aquae Sulis is unusual is that into the corner of the precinct projected the masonry enclosure surrounding the sacred spring and its reservoir. It was here that the waters of the main spring were retained within an irregularly planned lead-lined tank about three metres deep. The huge steaming reservoir, which later in its life was roofed with a masonry vault, was perhaps the most dramatic feature of the entire town. Standing by the altar it would have been possible to look into the reservoir enclosure and to glimpse, through the great windows in its far wall, the entrance hall of the baths beyond. Everything was arranged to create impressive and surprising vistas.

That visitors to Aquae Sulis flocked to the sacred spring is shown by the very considerable wear on the door sill leading into the enclosure. They came to view the waters and to make offerings to the goddess. When the spring and the drain leading from it were cleared out in the last century a large number of their votive offerings were found, including coins, brooches, a pin decorated with a pearl, a gold earring, a bag of thirty-three engraved gemstones, see colour slide (2), pewter plates and jugs, and a tin mask, see colour slide (3), thrown in by those who were either thanking the presiding deity for her favours or who were hopefully supporting their requests with gifts. Perhaps the most interesting of all the offerings was a small lead sheet about seven centimetres square, upon which had

QU(I) MIHI VILBIAM IN [V]OLAVIT SIC LUQUAT COM[O](DO) AQUA. ELL(A) MUTA QUI EAM V(OR)AVIT SI VELUINNA EXSUPEREUS VERIANUS SEVERINUS A[U]- GUSTALIS COMITIANUS CATUSMINIANUS GER- MANILL [A] IOVINA.

TRANSLATION
MAY HE WHO CARRIED OFF VILBIA FROM ME BECOME AS LIQUID AS WATER. (MAY) SHE WHO OBSCENELY DEVOURED HER (BECOME) DUMB, WHETHER VELVINNA, EXSUPEREUS, VERIANUS, SEVERINUS, A(U)GUSTALIS, COMITIANUS, CATUSMINIANUS, GERMANILLA (OR) JOVINA.

been scratched a curse backwards so that only the goddess could read it. It said quite simply 'May he who carried off Vilbia from me become as liquid as the waters' and then, for the goddess' information, a list of the possible culprits.

Some of the more wealthy visitors to the temple would have set up altars and other monuments to the glorification of gods. A number have been found in the temple, such as the two altars dedicated to the goddess Sulis for the welfare of and safety of Marcus Aufidius Maximus, a centurion of the sixth legion. One, shown on the next page, was put up by Aufidius Eutuches, the other by Marcus Aufidius Lemnus, both described as 'his freedman', in order to fulfil their vows. It may be that they erected these altars to him on the occasion of their being given their freedom.

Other, more impressive monuments were also constructed. One, known only from fragments recovered from beneath the Pump Room, represents the front of a building decorated with six regularly spaced

TO THE GODDESS SULIS FOR THE HEALTH AND SAFETY OF MARCUS AUFIDIUS MAXIMUS CENTURION OF THE SIXTH LEGION, AUFIDIUS EUTUCHES HIS FREEDMAN, WILLINGLY AND DESERVEDLY FULFILLED HIS VOW.

fluted pilasters or pillars. Between these were pairs of niches, the upper containing a cupid playing the part of a season, the lower representing a life-size seated figure, possibly also a season. The upper part of the wall was carved with a two-line inscription mentioning the goddess Sulis Minerva and implying that a local citizen, Claudius Ligur [   ], who may have been a member of a craft guild, was responsible for repairing and repainting 'at his own cost' an old building.

These are only a few of the offerings made by people to honour the goddess. Many more are known and there must be large numbers still to be recovered as further excavation becomes possible.

14

The baths

The second of the great buildings of Aquae Sulis is the bathing establishment which lies immediately to the south of the temple precinct. It is better known than the temple because from 1880 to 1896 and again in 1923 large areas of it were uncovered and much of the more impressive masonry is now on show to visitors. But it is only in recent years that we have come to understand the growth of the building and the way in which it was modified to suit changing needs. To begin with, the establishment was simple, consisting of three separate parts: a large entrance hall, three large swimming baths, the first entered through a door in the east wall of the hall, and a set of artificially heated baths west of the hall. A visitor would have entered the hall from the south. Once inside he would have been able to glimpse the sacred spring and the altar beyond through three huge windows set in the wall facing him. The hall itself, in addition to being a general place of assembly, would probably have been used as an apodyterium or undressing room. From here the bather would have proceeded to his chosen treatment. Turning west he would have passed into a suite of three rooms which together made up the equivalent of a Turkish bath. First of all he would have gone into the tepidarium or warm room which was heated by means of hot air circulating beneath the floor and passing up through hollow box-tiles set in the wall. A centrally heated floor of this kind, hollow beneath and supported on pillars of tiles, is known as a hypocaust. When his body had become acclimatised to the new temperature he would have gone into the caldarium or hot room next door, heated in the same way but to a much higher temperature. The caldarium was provided with two hot water baths opening out of recesses in its walls. They were heated by hot air circulating

15

Reconstruction of the great bath as it would have been in the third century; the room was roofed with a massive vault made of concrete and hollow boxtiles.

The interior of the great bath now; the round columns and the verandah roof are modern, colour slides (1) and (2).

beneath from a flue immediately outside, which also heated up the water in a bronze boiler set above it. These baths would probably have been of two different temperatures: the smaller, which was linked directly to the flue, being the hotter. It was in the sweating atmosphere of the caldarium that the bather's body would have been scraped with a curved instrument, called a strigil, to remove sweat and dirt. After this the bather would have re-entered the tepidarium, staying there long enough to allow his body to cool gradually. He may then have decided to take a quick swim in the natatio or cold swimming bath nearby before returning to the entrance hall.

For visitors requiring a less rigorous relaxation, the east end of the establishment provided the answer, for here were three large swimming baths filled with hot mineral water channelled in straight from the

17

spring. The first chamber, which contained the great bath, was by far the most impressive—a rectangular room 34 metres by 20 metres containing a large lead-lined swimming bath 2 metres deep, colour slides (4) and (5). Flanking the long sides of the bath were two arcades which served to divide off the side passages from the bath itself, and opening out of the walls of these side walks were rectangular and semicircular alcoves where onlookers could sit.

Above the main arcades there would have been a second storey in which were set a series of large windows to provide light, for it must be remembered that the room was completely roofed in at this stage. Beyond the chamber containing the great bath was a smaller room with a bath set in the centre of its floor and another in an alcove opening out of its east wall. Since these were fed directly from the great bath they must have been somewhat cooler. This, then, is the bathing establishment as it was first built sometime towards the end of the first century AD. What followed in later centuries was merely an extension of the original facilities.

The first alterations, made in the second century, are of some interest. To begin with, a new circular hot room, known as a laconicum, was built to provide an atmosphere of intense dry heat similar to the modern sauna baths. With this type of treatment two further facilities were required: a cold plunge bath for a quick dousing immediately following the heat treatment, and an exercise court in which the bather could tire himself before bathing. A careful examination of the plan shows clearly how the necessary modifications were made. The centre part of the entrance hall was partitioned off and a large circular bath was inserted into the floor to provide the cold plunge, colour slide (6). This was linked by corridors to the laconicum, while to the south part of the earlier arrangement was converted into a large exercise courtyard. Thus the visitor could now choose between a swim in the thermal waters, a steaming Turkish bath or the invigorating sauna-type treatment.

At about this time alterations were also carried out at the east end where the old swimming bath was removed and replaced by another set of Turkish baths. Why the establishment now possessed two suites of baths poses interesting problems. However, at this time it was unfashionable for men and women to bathe together. Baths were opened on different days, or at different times of day, for the two sexes. It is possible that the arrangement at Aquae Sulis provided facilities for men at one end and women at the other, so that the baths could remain open all the time.

The hot thermal waters that were such an attraction at the baths also posed problems, for soon the timbers of the main roofs began to warp seriously. Eventually the decision was taken to re-roof the circular bath, the great bath and the bath next to it in masonry. The other baths of the artificially heated suites were already roofed in this manner, largely to prevent the risk of fire from sparks from the furnaces and hypocausts. The re-roofing of the main chambers on such a scale was an enormous undertaking, largely because masonry was so much heavier than the timber roof for which the building had originally been designed. This meant that all the foundation work had to be strengthened. The arcade piers, for example, were increased in size by the addition of large pilasters to the front and back faces, new pilasters were added to the corners of the alcoves and elsewhere walls were strengthened with blind arcades, that is arches added to the front of a wall which had already been built resulting in the doubling of its strength without an equivalent loss of space. These alterations can all be traced amid the ruins today. The vaults were built of hollow box-tiles to reduce the weight and were open at the ends to allow the steam to escape. Fragments now preserved in the baths show these features clearly.

The later history of the baths saw further extensions and rebuildings, leading to bigger and better facilities for bathers. The Turkish suites were completely remodelled on a grand scale and elsewhere specialised

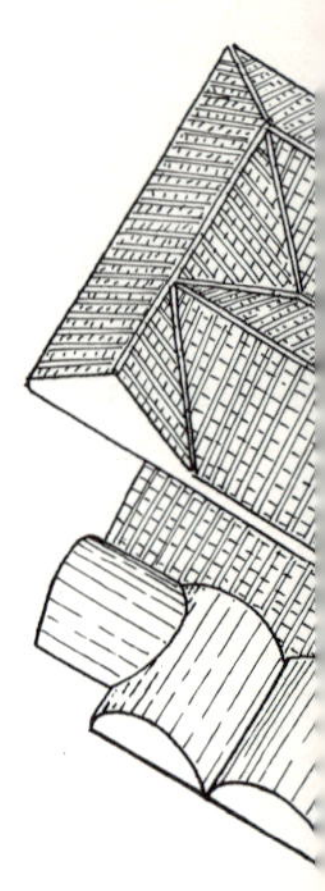

Reconstruction of the baths as they would have been in the third century AD; the labelling on the diagram relates to this period.

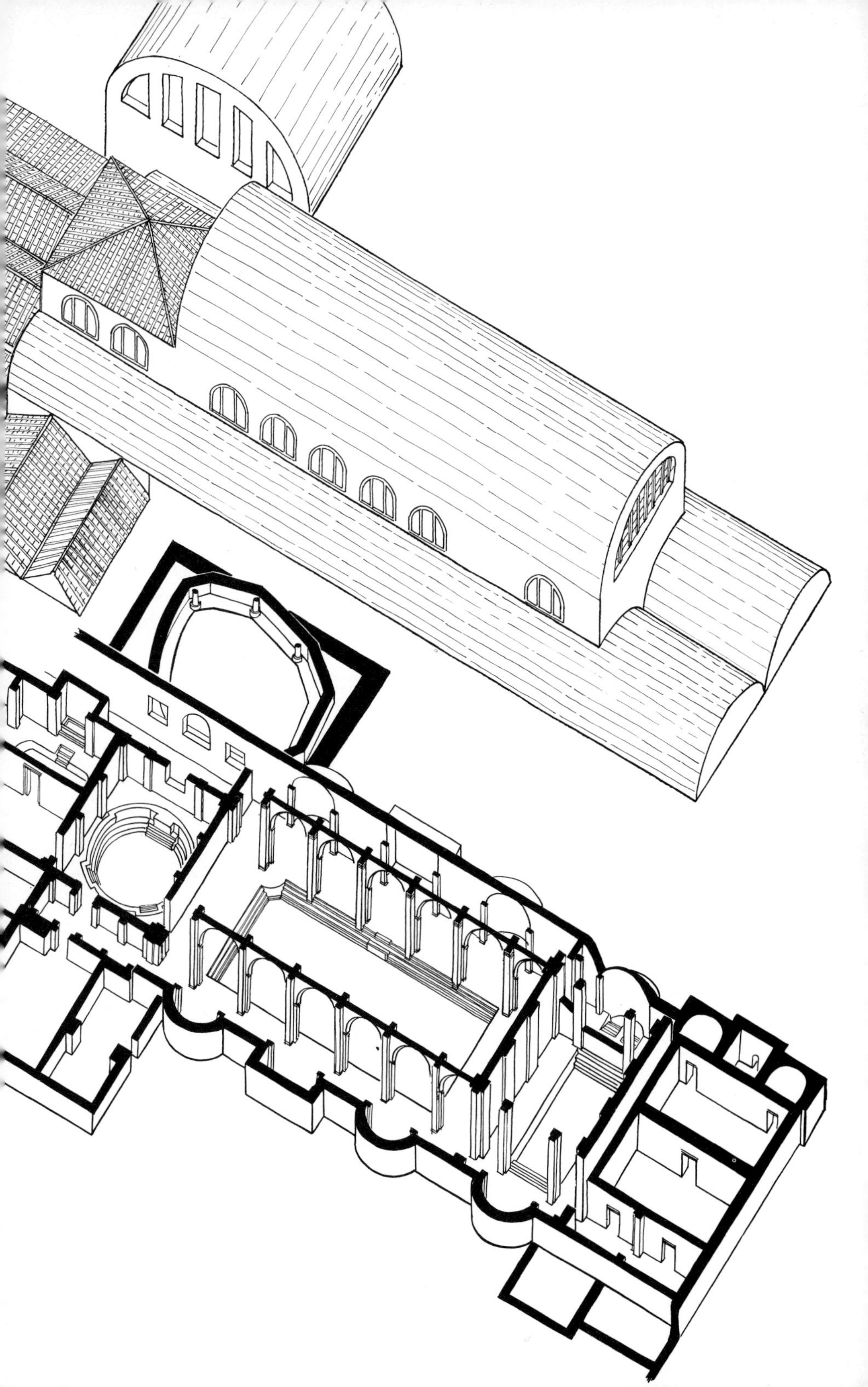

immersion and curative baths were constructed to cater for the infirm. One of these can be seen now in the alcove on the north side of the bath beyond the great bath to the east. Here the floor of the alcove was lowered and a stone seat built around the wall so that the sick could sit down immersed up to the neck in curative water. The Emperor Augustus is said to have been cured of a serious disease by just such a treatment. The water for this bath was provided by a lead pipe running directly from the reservoir. A considerable length of the pipe still survives in position. It was made in lengths of 3 metres from flat sheets beaten into a circular or triangular section and fused along the edge. Each section was carefully slotted into the next and molten lead poured over the junction to make a watertight seal. Enormous quantities of lead were used in the baths, not only for piping but also for lining all the baths. The great bath still retains its original lead sheeting.

From the above description it will be clear that the development of the bathing establishment was elaborately and expensively carried out. It demonstrates forcefully the power, vitality and wealth of the civic authorities.

One further building in this central complex deserves mention. It lies north of the baths and east of the temple, in the area now below the museum and the abbey, and is represented now by several substantial masonry footings. From its position it could be one of two possible structures: either it is the forum or the stage area of a theatre. Both arrangements are well represented on the continent. In this context, however, in a town the size of Aquae Sulis it is more likely to be a theatre, since a monumental forum would have been out of place in such a small settlement. Theatres laid out on the same axis as a temple occur frequently in the Roman world and serve as a reminder that theatrical performances were often an essential part of religious ceremonies. Only further excavation beneath the abbey, at present impossible, would solve the problem.

Besides the central public buildings, what would the rest of the Roman town have been like? While there are many scraps of evidence available, the picture is still far from clear. It is not known for certain whether or not the medieval town wall followed a Roman predecessor. Everything points to the fact that it did, but conclusive proof is still lacking. If so, the walled area was very small, only 9 hectares compared with more than 40 hectares for the average Roman county town, and much of this would have been taken up with the great central buildings. There were also several other bathing and religious sites within the walled area. Another spring rose in the south-west corner (now the hot bath spring); it too was provided

Mosaic pavement found originally in a Roman house in the north-west corner of the town, now relaid in the Roman baths

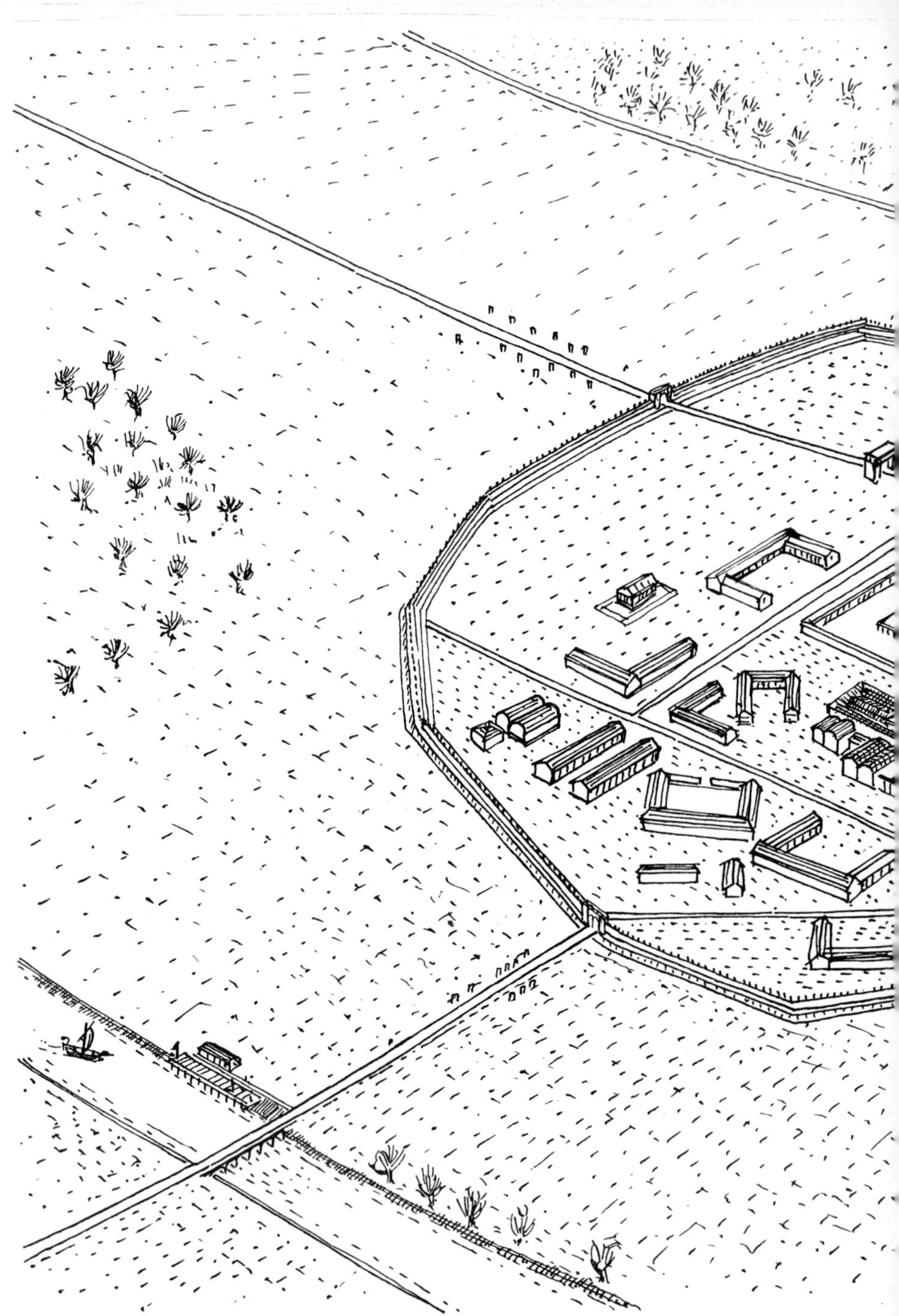

Aquae Sulis as it may have looked in the third century: the baths and the temple lay in the centre of the walled area. Other buildings

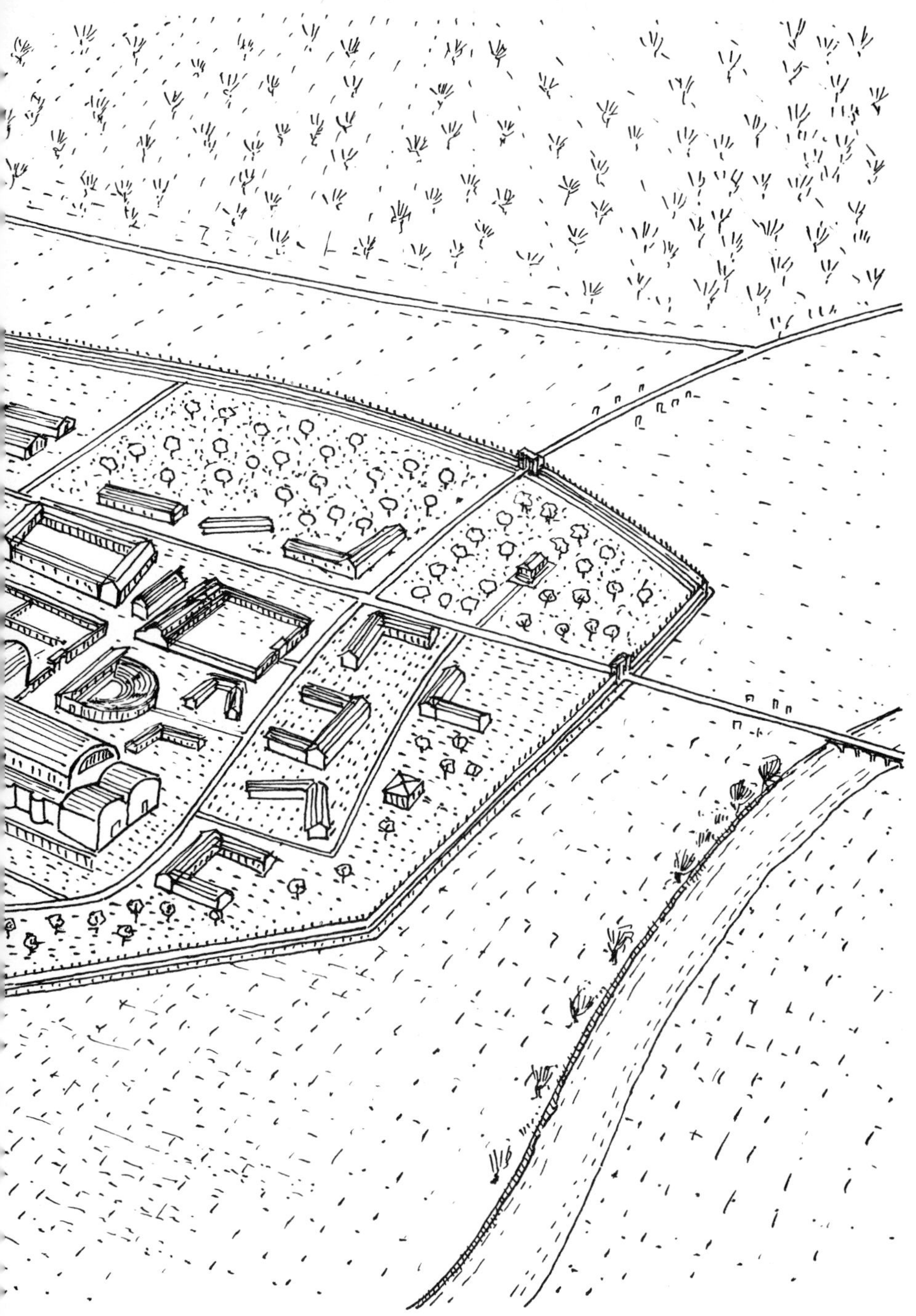

including smaller baths, shrines and town houses were scattered haphazardly around.

with a bathing establishment of some size which incorporated a lead-lined swimming bath. A little to the north another spring (now the cross bath spring) seems to have served a sacred cistern into which, later, several carved and inscribed stones had fallen. Finally, somewhere in this part of the town was 'the sacred place' referred to on one of several altars found in the middle of the eighteenth century. Exactly where it was cannot now be discovered.

Between this densely packed jumble of religious and bathing establishments were the private houses, the hotels and the shops which a tourist centre of this importance must have possessed. Parts of at least ten houses of some size, many with fine mosaics, have been found from time to time, but there is still a great lack of knowledge as to the town plan, in fact not a single Roman street has yet with certainty been uncovered. Our lack of knowledge can be ascribed to the fine quality of the eighteenth century building and its slow rate of replacement.

The people of Aquae Sulis

So far we have been mainly concerned with the buildings of the Roman town, for they, after all, provide the most tangible evidence of the past, but fortunately there is another source of information—inscriptions—which enable us to look more closely at the people who lived in and visited the town. The great bathing establishment, the temple and the theatre (?) would together have formed one of the finest complexes of public buildings in Aquae Sulis. The fame of the hot springs and their curative properties spread throughout the Roman world, attracting large numbers of visitors. Most of them, by the very nature of the evidence, must remain anonymous but the names of some are recorded either on altars which they erected to the gods after, or in anticipation of, the deities' support, or on tombstones put up by relatives after, perhaps, the curative properties of the waters had proved unsuccessful.

Several of the inscriptions record foreign visitors. One, a tombstone, was erected for a middle-aged lady, Rusonia Aventina, who belonged to the tribe of the Mediomatrici near Metz. She died at the age of fifty-eight and was buried in one of the cemeteries by her heir, Lucius Sestius, perhaps a relation who had travelled with her from Europe. Another distant traveller was Perigrinus, son of Secundus, who came from the area around modern Trier. He erected an altar to two of his favourite patron gods, Loucetius Mars and Nemetona, who were in origin Celtic deities worshipped frequently on the northern and western fringes of the Empire.

Not all the visitors were necessarily attracted solely by the springs. Priscus, son of Toutius, who travelled all the way from the region of Chartres, styles himself lapidarius (a stone worker). In all probability he came to Aquae Sulis to look at the superb building stone available in the neighbourhood, unless of course he had already settled in the town. We know more of another stone mason—Sulinus, son of Brucetus, whose altar was dedicated to the local deities, the Suleviae. The same man put up an altar to the same gods in Corinium (Cirencester). This particular inscription was found in 1899, together with eight other sculptured stones, mostly in an unweathered condition. Some people have suggested that this was in fact the mason's yard belonging to Sulinus and that he travelled to Aquae Sulis in order to purchase a load of Bath stone. While this may be true, we shall never know for certain.

Local dignitaries from other Romano-British towns journeyed to Aquae Sulis to take the waters—an eighty-year-old decurion (town councillor) from Glevum (Gloucester) is recorded on one inscription and there must have been many others whose presence has passed un-noted. It was popular too with soldiers. Some of them like Vitellius Tancinus, mentioned on page 3, may have been stationed in or near Aquae

Sulis. The same was probably true of Marcus Valerius Latinus of the XX legion. Others, however, were more likely to be visitors or veterans who chose the spa as a suitable place for their retirement. One of the visiting soldiers, Julius Vitalis, an armourer of the XX legion who had been recruited from Gallia Belgica died after only nine years of service at the age of twenty-nine, probably from some crippling disease. His tombstone records that he belonged to a craft guild to which he would have contributed part of his pay. When he died there were sufficient funds available to pay for his cremation and his tombstone, upon which is inscribed the phrase 'with funeral at the cost of the Guild of Armourers'.

Other soldiers were evidently settlers—men like Marcus Aufidius Maximus, the centurion of the VI legion who freed two of his slaves. Another soldier, whose name is not recorded, lost his bronze diploma just outside Aquae Sulis—diplomas were issued to all soldiers on their retirement. This particular example recorded that the man had served in the Ala I Gallorum Proculeiana early in the second century and had, after twenty-five years of service, been granted citizenship. Like a large number of retired veterans, he would have chosen some congenial place in which to settle down with his family—there must have been many such men living in and about the towns of Roman Britain, some of them perhaps setting up as traders or artisans, others becoming small farmers.

These are just a few of the people who lived in the town or visited it during the Roman period: altogether more than forty are known by name, mainly from inscriptions or tombstones. What type of men they were and why they came to the spa we shall never know for certain, but it is most unlikely that they would have missed a morning or afternoon at the baths, swimming gently in the hot waters of the great bath or taking one of the more specialised heat treatments and then resting in the entrance hall where they would have met their friends and talked at leisure. The rest of the day might have been spent in the temple, watching a sacrifice being carried out on the great altar, then perhaps visiting the sacred spring and throwing some trinket into the water for luck. In the temple precinct a visitor would have met many different groups of people: souvenir sellers, physicians selling ointments and medicines, builders repairing and repainting old buildings and perhaps a little family ceremony dedicating a small altar to the goddess for some favour. After this he may have attended a religious performance in the theatre next door and then returned for dinner in the private houses of friends or in the mansio or hotel in which he may have been staying. All the time, however, it must be remembered that tourist activities were only one part of the scene —the everyday life of the town must have continued as it did in most of the other urban centres.

The cemeteries

The cemeteries of the settlement are fairly well known, with burials occurring on practically every side of the town, but the main cemetery lay to the north along the line of the Fosse Way, now the London Road. For the last four hundred years burials and tombstones have turned up, ranging from the simplest cremations or inhumations, located perhaps only by a simple timber marker, to elaborately carved masonry tombs like the one to which the fine relief of a mastiff carrying a dead stag across his back, shown on page 30, belongs. One of the most dramatic of the tombs incorporated a greater-than-life sized head of a woman sculpted in stone and now in the museum, see page 30. Her hair-style is typical of those fashionable in the late first century. Between these extremes were the more usual tombstones, of which a number survive. One deserves particular mention here: it is a simple stone, piously carved in the form of an altar, put up to the memory of a seventy-five year old priest of the goddess Sulis called Gaius Calpurnius. It was

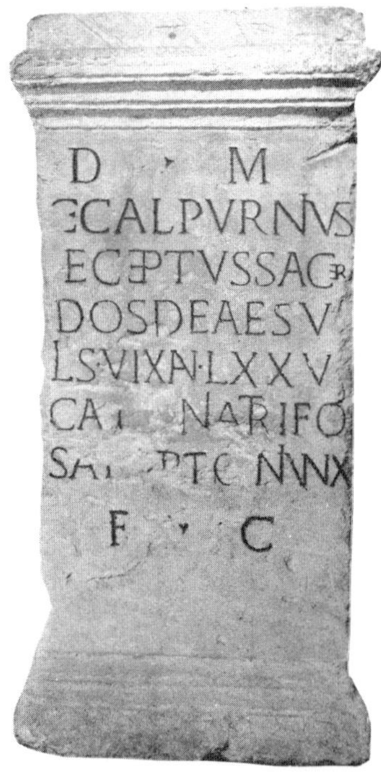

*Three tombstones:
top, relief of a mastiff
carrying a slaughtered
deer; below, left, sculp-
tured head of a lady; below,
right, the tombstone of Gaius
Calpurnius.*

TO THE SPIRITS OF THE DEPARTED:
GAIUS CALPURNIUS RECEPTUS,
PRIEST OF THE GODDESS SULIS,
LIVED 75 YEARS; CALPURNIA
TRIFOSA, HIS FREEDWOMAN AND
WIFE, HAD THIS SET UP.

erected by his wife, originally his slave, Calpurnia
Trifosa. This simple stone symbolises much of the
life and death of Aquae Sulis.

The discussion so far will have given a picture of the
Roman settlement as a place unlike the normal
county town—a settlement essentially specialised

30

towards its spa and its tourist industry. This is largely true but it must also be remembered that Aquae Sulis lay in the centre of a rich area of countryside, admirably served by good communications. Moreover, it is an area without a natural economic centre other than the town. Aqua Sulis, then, must have developed commercial overtones not only as a market centre for the farm produce from the countryside but also for more specialised commodities such as the pewter manufactured at Camerton to the south and Lansdown to the north. Pewter vessels and plates became popular during the fourth century AD as a substitute for the extortionately priced silverware. The freestone of the region was also highly prized and it can hardly be by accident that two visiting stone-masons, Sulinus and Priscus, are recorded on inscriptions found in the town. Commercial activity, religious celebration and pleasure were closely associated in the Roman world with much the same spirit as that behind the medieval fair. Aquae Sulis, by virtue of its economic position and natural and man-made facilities, was admirably suited for such a combination of functions.

Later history

While the early development of the town is rather obscure, it is possible with some precision to describe its end. The first sign of unrest is recorded on an altar put up by Gaius Severius Emeritus, who boasts that he 'restored and cleansed afresh . . . this holy spot wrecked by insolent hands'. It is difficult to know what to make of this, but one context may lie in the events following the early fourth century, when Christianity was legalised and over-zealous Christians smashed some of the old Pagan shrines. Within half a century or so, however, paganism revived.

The real trouble began with the increasing severity of the Avon floods which may have been linked in some way to the rise in sea-level experienced by much of Western Europe from the third century onwards. The first hint of this in the baths is given by the raising of some of the hypocaust basement floors, but even this was not sufficient, for sometime in the fourth century several of the hypocausts were flooded, leaving a thick silt deposit which can still be traced among the pilae upon which the floors were supported. A temporary solution was found in raising the floors yet again by ramming clay between the supports, but still the floods came and eventually, late in the fourth century, the baths and the low lying areas of the temple precinct were abandoned to the flood waters, augmented by the still vigorous springs. However, the town was not abandoned. Occupation continued and household rubbish including animal bones and broken pottery was thrown into the rising marsh. The recent excavations beneath the Pump Room cellars, over the area of the temple precinct, demonstrated this vividly showing that some 40 centimetres of mud had formed whilst the rubbish tipping proceeded. Pollen and spores from the mud belonged to bracken, mosses and other bog-loving species.

Elsewhere in the town urban life seems to have thrived for a while. One site excavated recently in Abbeygate Street showed how a masonry building of some quality built late in the third century, and subsequently modified, was allowed to fall down only to be replaced later by what appears to be an even more substantial structure, which must date to the early fifth century. But gradually standards declined with the break-down of Roman economy and government and the onset of Saxon and Irish raids.

During this time the vaults of the baths and temple collapsed and subsided into the muddy waters, leaving only the walls and piers still projecting from the marsh. Town life must have continued in some shadowy way, for at the time of the famous Saxon victory at Dyrham in 577 Aquae Sulis is mentioned together with Glevum and Corinium (Cirencester) as passing into the hands of the conquerors.